VESUVIUS

Adare McAllis

Two letters by Pliny the Younger
to the historian Cornelius Tacitus
regarding the death of Pliny the Elder
and the survival of himself and his mother
after the famous eruption in the year 79 of

VESUVIUS

In a new translation by Kenneth Martin
With illustrations by Adare McAllister
Designed and edited by Gary Miller

IRON BEAR
· PRESS ·

San Diego · 2008

Printed in the United States of America

First published in paperback in February 2008

ISBN 978-0-6151-9131-7

Iron Bear Press
Post Office Box 90340
San Diego, California 92169

www.ironbearpress.com

CONTENTS

Aut quid non miraculo est
cum primum in notitiam venit.

—C. Plini Secundi
Nat. Hist. lib. vii cap. 6

And in fact what is not marvelous
when it first comes to notice.

—Pliny the Elder
Natural History, Bk. VII, Ch. 6

INTRODUCTION

In Roman antiquity adoption within extended families was more than an act of charity or a curious point of personal history. There are modern arrangements, nonetheless, that approximate in purpose and outcome the ancient partiality of promoting, for example, nephews' interests through adoption by their uncles. Among these, Andrew Jackson's rearing of three nephews stands out, even if only one of the boys went on to a distinguished career. Similar in spirit also to the old practice was the adoption by one Thomas Hancock, a rich and influential lawyer, of his orphaned nephew John, whose future as a rich lawyer Thomas assured, while the nephew's influence lingers on in the aura his signature emits from off a renowned document. Such association between uncle and nephew in pre-Christian Europe, though, might take on mythical proportions.

Politicians famously valued avuncular or at least non-filial descent at the time of the Roman Empire, for the practice let powerful sonless men identify successors with whom they were well acquainted and whose characters they had most likely helped to mold. When, for instance, Julius Caesar adopted by will his sister Julia's great-nephew Octavian, the invincible general bestowed an advantage if not a supremacy on the young man who would become *Augustus* seventeen years after the uncle's assassination. In less admirably all-in-the family fashion, this Caesar Augustus while still alive allowed a stepson to follow him in the principate, and his adoptee Tiberius arranged to keep the Empire from persons he deemed unsatisfactory by designating out of caprice and paranoia his second wife's step-grandson, the unconscionable Caligula, who descended linearly from Augustus himself.

But the process of intrafamilial adoption in Rome could promote ends other than political expediency or calamitous imperial succession. This is the happy case with two northern Italians, Gaius Plinius Secundus and his nephew Publius Caecilius Secundus, who upon the former's death exchanged his first name for the *praenomen* of his adopter and inserted the older man's gentile name into his own, thereby becoming in accordance with Roman custom Gaius Plinius Caecilius Secundus. These Plinius and Caecilius *gentes* or clans were prosperous landowners around Lake Larius in cisalpine Gaul, today known as Lake Como in upper Lombardy, and the clever of their male offspring followed stereotypical paths into prosperity through legal advocacy and senatorial election. Although participating broadly in public life and indeed serving two sovereigns by administering distant provinces of the Empire, the Plinius relatives who in the Middle Ages would become known as Pliny the Elder and

Pliny the Younger engaged life most fully not in litigation or power brokering but by talent and inclination in reading and writing. Moreover, prior to their shared if short-lived joy of learning was the pleasure of shared origins and individual benefaction to their hometown Comum, the Italian *Como*, a kind of antipodes of beauty to that region of their lives' highest drama, the Bay of Naples.

Before the younger Pliny became legally the son of Pliny the Elder upon his uncle's death by asphyxiation on the shores of that bay in 79 CE, he had spent years with his mother's brother, for his father died when he was very young, and it was probably this kinsman who, when the emperor Vespasian offered him in the early 70s a series of procuratorships, or offices of civil administration reporting directly to the emperor, took along to Rome his eleven-year-old nephew and there initiated the boy's formal education. Accordingly, Pliny the Younger enjoyed the abundance of his uncle's distinguished mind a decade at least before he inherited his huge fortune. The intellectual wealth on its own was substantial. Pliny the Elder, a polymath and prolific author, composed voluminous works, all now lost, on contemporary history; these were esteemed in antiquity, but he was best known during his lifetime for the encyclopedic knowledge and inexhaustible energy that enabled him to produce thirty-seven books of natural history. This stupendous work, the largest of its kind hitherto and called *Naturalis Historia*, has survived intact, and not least of its words' importance must be their contribution to the understanding of Latin today, since by leafing through any source-based lexicon one discovers that the citation "PLIN.*Nat.*" occurs by far more than any other.

The adolescent nephew Pliny, as is obvious from his attitude in the two letters that comprise this book, admired the illustrious relative and his achievements, and it would appear, for sure, that on August 24, 79, he was Uncle Gaius's diligent protégé. When he came to write his account of the horrific day twenty-five years after the fact—the sole eyewitness report extant of the eruption of Mount Vesuvius—Pliny the Younger could only lament how it was unquenchable curiosity that had got the better of his very learned (*eruditissimus*) uncle, since the gentleman was determined to see for himself close up the great thing that had to be known (*magnum noscendum*) and so sailed away to his death.

*   *   *

Despite an evident fondness for his uncle, Pliny the Younger comes across on first acquaintance as rather the opposite of him in mind and temperament. The impression, however, is misleading because, though choosing to stay at home and read when he could have witnessed for himself what turned out to be the most fabulous natural disaster ever fabled by humankind, the younger Pliny's subsequent career as referenced in history and revealed preponderantly in ten books of published letters was filled with event, marked by some courage, and largely enjoyed. If he appears to a modern reader an unadventurous or even spiritless youth at age seventeen, one need only remember how not so very uncommon it is that a sensitive lad with a bookish bent and concomitant tendency to priggishness should find strength and purpose and make something of himself, whether sooner or later.

4

For Pliny the nephew the finding was sooner, as he was already pursuing by his mid twenties the prescribed *cursus honorum* or path of public offices, a ladder to luster that all ambitious, well-placed men of class climbed in the Rome of the Republic and Empire. By his early thirties, Pliny the Younger held a high reputation for arguing cases in the civil courts of the capital and for doing so in exemplary oratorical Latin, which he liked to declaim before a circle of friends in the way of rehearsal. By 90 he had entered the senate, and in 100 at age thirty-nine he attained a consulship; thereafter, the emperor Trajan favored him with various administrative appointments until he was sent as *legatus Augusti*, ambassador plenipotentiary of the sovereign, to the strategically important but at the time badly ruled province of Bithynia-Pontus, what is now northwestern Turkey. There he was to die, probably in 112, but not before he restored some semblance of order to the troubled region and formulated a policy of official conduct vis-à-vis the new, disturbing, and fast spreading sect of estranged people who called themselves Christians. Indeed, one of the reasons for Pliny the Younger's enduring prestige into and beyond the Middle Ages lies in his generally indulgent and humane dealings with these inspired folk. He details in distressed letters to the emperor his perplexity of how to treat with the Christians and wonders if he is doing right by them and right, of course, by Rome. Trajan's rescripts, whose import the younger Pliny paraphrases in his letters about the problem, are full of assurance and praise for the legate's tact.

Proficiency in the law, in diplomacy, and, so far as it is known, in his domestic life appears to be the hallmark of this Roman, but Pliny the Younger's reputation for it would probably not have been so remarkable as to survive if it was not for the mastery he attained in the quite ordinary occupation of letter writing, which was practiced then by almost all cultivated gentlemen. The singular charm of the younger Pliny's prose derives, first off, from a huge menu of matter: he recounts senatorial debates, business deals, crop failures, and testamentary disputes, but he also shares with correspondents his opinions on the decline of rhetoric, thoughts about the restoration of a temple, thanks for a gift of two "very beautiful" thrushes, advice on interpreting a bad dream, disparagement of a friend who broke a dinner engagement, and, as well, remarks on the paradise of his Tuscan villa, the brave death of an old lady, a haunted house in Athens, and the coarse witticisms of a crude entertainer. All this, the stuff of existence apprehended by a lively mind, would have delighted the younger Pliny's readers then and can only amaze them now, for the letters detail the life of a typical, fortune-favored embodiment of first-century thought and conduct.

Beside the inherent appeal of the topics, it is Pliny the Younger's adult personality that has won him readers for two thousand years. At once thoughtful and jovial, upstanding and political, generous and efficient, striving and self-deprecating, he disarms his audience with a sensibility that may be *haut bourgeois* but is, one feels, always genuine. Moreover, the manner of his verbal expression seems so appropriate to his disposition: ancient grammarians and commentators praise him for using the "commonest" nouns with the "most essential" qualifiers; they note, too, as if commenting on an exertion of refinement, a cunning arrangement of words within highly structured sentences. The noticeable cleverness of composition, though, seldom tires today by its noticeability and, except when occasionally obscure, often beguiles. But no matter—any buzzing belletristic quality obtrudes hardly at all in face of the momentous content that the second Pliny styles into shape for his two most famous letters.

The writer was a mature man when he put together for Tacitus reminiscences of the awful hours and days that followed the eruption of Vesuvius. Pliny the Younger's work had been concerned more or less with current events till the historian's request, and his imagination dwelt most congenially on ephemera; he had written about individuals' deaths, it is true, and once about a suicide, but he never assayed subjects involving massive misfortune or social unpleasantness of any sort, and he would have had plenty of opportunity to do so during the latter part of Vespasian's reign. Would it have been difficult for such a sanguine soul, buffered by great wealth and canny political correctness, to fulfill Tacitus's requirement (*exigenti*) and to face even so long afterward the pain that events connected with the explosion of the volcano, primarily the death of his beloved uncle, must have occasioned? The only hint of such difficulty is the author's intake of deep breath, as it were, before he begins the second of the letters, and he manages this with a literary, distancing reference to the archetypal Roman hero Aeneas, who also had trouble starting a story (see the beginning of Book II of Vergil's *Aeneid*).

The reader senses, in any case, that the middle-aged writer when revisiting the grievous scene feels shame before his initial nonchalance but satisfaction before the challenges he assumes just a few hours later, that the older man understands and respects the needling necessity of youth to be brave. Whatever emotions the nephew Pliny internalized in order to satisfy his friend Tacitus, he had indeed risen to a certain test of character at age seventeen when he jeopardized his own survival to insure that of his mother. He knew later on that he had so risen; a modest pride in this accomplishment can be appreciated in the careful Latin of his sentences.

*   *   *

With a vocabulary half as plentiful as that of English, Latin must make do with more significations per word than English and with many more inflectional endings: make do it does, and well, by effecting an extreme concision of thought in sentences of remarkably free word order. If the genius of written English tells less by the placement of words in a sentence, because this aspect of its grammar is so arbitrary, the bounty of written Latin lies not in quantity of available words but in the purity of their use and the ingenuity of their arrangement. Accordingly, the challenge before a translator of Latin into English is twofold: first, to decide the meaning of a sentence with its basic sense informed by words' etymology and context and with its full sense qualified by the overtones of the words' diction; second, to determine which syntactical endowments of the primary language when replicated might enhance, or will defy, transfer of meaning to the targeted tongue.

Since it is a translation of Pliny's thought in these two

letters and not a synopsis or summary of it to which this version aspires—to as comprehensive a rendering as possible of Pliny's meaning—"how" questions like these occur continually: how to get in English both the succinctness of a rather simple Latin sentence and capture, for instance, the emphasis that the author has placed by word order on its direct object? how to retain in a difficult Latin sentence the importance, say, of the writer's repeated present participles in different oblique cases and the implications of its three dependent clauses, each of which slightly contradicts the others? how to reconcile two tenses in a pretty straightforward Latin sentence without losing in English the effect of Pliny's very deliberate mixing of them? how to reproduce in English the author's purposeful disregard of temporal sequence in the apodosis of a past contrafactual condition and pick up the finesse of the ablative absolute that begins the sentence? how to eke out a straightforward interpretation of a meteorological description while avoiding verbal inflation of one hundred fifty percent?

Addressing this last question may cast a helpful light on the accommodations translators make with their authors. A comparison of three versions of a relatively straightforward sentence from the first letter published in this volume (Book VI, Letter 16, Chapter 5) will elucidate how even a simple factual matter—smoke coming from a mountaintop—can involve gnarly trade-offs between style and content when Englishing Pliny's Latin. The original of the twenty-four-word sentence,

Nubes—incertum procul intuentibus ex quo monte (Vesuvium fuisse postea cognitum est)—oriebatur, cuius

similitudinem et formam non alia magis arbor quam pinus expresserit,

may be rendered brutally in thirty-three English words:

A cloud—uncertain to watchers from afar from what mountain (Vesuvius it was learned afterward to have been)—was rising, whose likeness and shape no other tree more than a stone-pine would have expressed.

Here is a fifty-one-word translation by the flamboyant British colonial governor and author of *The Last Days of Pompeii*, Edward Bulwer-Lytton:

The cloud was to be seen gradually rising upwards, though from the great distance it was uncertain from which of the mountains it arose; it was afterwards, however, ascertained to be Vesuvius. In appearance and shape it strongly resembled a tree; perhaps it was more like a pine than anything else, . . .

Over one hundred sixty years later in 1997 a professor at Amherst College, Cynthia Damon, rendered this Pliny in thirty-five words:

The cloud was rising from a mountain—at such a distance we couldn't tell which, but afterwards learned that it was Vesuvius. I can best describe its shape by likening it to a pine tree.

The finished translation from page 25 below takes thirty-seven English words:

A cloud—to those watching at a distance it was uncertain from what mountain, but later it was learned to have been Vesuvius—was rising. Its shape resembled a stone-pine more than any other tree.

The rhetorical appeal of the middle versions above is

readily apparent. In the case of Bulwer-Lytton's rendition, the pleonasm of "rising upwards," the contrast of "uncertain" with "ascertained," the dubious distinction of "appearance" and "shape" (actually a Latin hendiadys) please with their implicit judgment of Pliny as casual and artless (well, the thing *was* sort of like a pine tree); moreover, "which of the mountains" and "from the great distance" suggest Pliny was all about picture painting in his account of the calamity, and truly this long Victorian sentence offers the reader an effect of panning cinematically across a landscape before zooming in on some outrage, climatic or criminal. Pliny comes across here as curious and insouciant, a gentleman whom the famously intemperate Bulwer-Lytton may have envied.

Damon, on the other hand, has her Pliny eschew any affinity for pretty scenery but rather grants him scientific sureness: she has Pliny declare as "best" his comparison of the smoke issuing from Vesuvius to a "pine tree." Moreover, she would have Pliny determine the distance across the Bay of Naples as "such" and that a "pine tree" is a pine tree is a pine tree, for why should C. Plinius Caecilius Secundus vouchsafe redundant information to a clueless reader? Damon's Pliny wishes to insure an appearance of veracity—"we" corroborates even Pliny's uncertainty and, thereby, all his testimony—and a commitment to brisk authority includes even a contraction in negating a modal verb ("couldn't").

The fact that verbal facts simply do not occur in the Latin lying before Bulwer-Lytton and Damon cannot be allowed to detract from the two translators' accomplishment. How, for instance, does Bulwer-Lytton know that the smoke from Vesuvius rises "gradually" without that adverb explicit in the original? Answer: the deponent verb *orior* often seems to mean "appear above" or "arise," as in "emerge." Where does Damon get the right to inject the first person into her rendering of this sentence? Answer: Pliny earlier talked much about himself and others collectively, and so the reader must infer, Damon implies, that the details of Pliny's account are all first-hand; in the case of *cognitum est*, any passive construction naturally implies an agent, which here can only be "I" or "we."

The consideration of what to infer and confer, to include and exclude, while presuming to bring out yet another version of famous writing weighs heavily in the translation of the two letters below. Pliny knew, of course, from the air he breathed that Latin's arsenal of rhetorical strategies or figures of speech was immense even for prose and that meaning emerged from a group of words as much by their grouping as by their signification and syntax. An awareness of his sure knowledge of these truths directs the linguistic and literary decisions taken with regard to this new translation.

In the "brutal" and "finished" versions, for instance, of the working example concerned with a cloud, the general policy that is applied throughout these renderings of letters vi.16 and vi.20 may be seen: adherence, arguably to a fault, to Latin word order and succinctness of English idiom, verging on the laconic, to match that of the original. Hence, the em-dashed explanation between *nubes* and *oriebatur* in order to capture the suspense of "a cloud" (enhanced further by repeating the indefinite article "a" instead of, as normal in translation of Latin, articling with "the" an already named entity)—what was it doing? why was it there?—and its activity ("was rising"). Hence, too, an attempt to capture the super-compressed Latin of *non alia magis arbor quam pinus* with "a stone-pine more than any other tree." The reader may well ask why the "brutal" version of the second sentence cannot have served as the final one, since there are more than mere glimmers of sense in its awkward English: the answer must be that it is just too brutal, seeing how, outside of poetry, trees in English do not "express" or even possess perceptions, nor can English assume a prolepsis in comparison as severe as "no other tree" when nothing at all, let alone a tree, has yet been hinted at as a "likeness" to the cloud. The "brutal" translation would make a good crib for the lazy student, but it would not do for the purposes of rendering clearly and smoothly continuous prose narrative.

*　　*　　*

To give the illatinate or rustilated reader an insight into the diversity of design at the original author's disposal when telling his exciting story, here are a few conspicuous schemes and tools by which Pliny breathes life into his narrative, *not* by which he adds to or ornaments the narrative, since Pliny is too good a writer, even with occasional figurative excess, to "use" style in his prose. The examples are restricted to those figures which are little employed in English (as opposed to metaphor, personification, irony, sentence length, etc. which are omnipresent in both written languages) and which challenged this translator the most. For convenience of access, the figures are discussed with reference to whether they are operative at word or sentence level.

Some examples at word level

Alliteration, the repetition of sound at the beginning of contiguous words: *mali motus*, the evil's motion (vi. 16. 10); *tremor terrae*, trembling of the earth (vi. 20. 3); *metu mortis mortem*, in fear of death, death (vi. 20. 14); *flammae flammarumque*, flames and flames' (vi. 16. 18)—the initial consonants help forebode disaster; polyptoton (cf. infra) strengthens the last two examples.

Anaphora, repetition of a word at the beginning of contiguous phrases, clauses, or sentences: *illud ruisse, illud ardere*, this part was collapsing, this part was burning (vi. 20. 15)—the town's particular districts are singled out for horror; *iam hora diei prima ... iam quassatis*, now dawn ... now with shaken (vi. 20. 6)—the repetition of "now" ... "now" is like a wrecking ball, and the lack of parallel construction in the grammar between "now it was dawn" and "with shaken (buildings)" disorients the reader in the way the chaos around the escapees must have discomfited them.

Antithesis, juxtaposition or mixing of contrary or unexpected ideas, persons, or sentiments: *in pavore simile prudentiae*, in a state of terror similar to prudence (vi. 20. 7)—the antithesis startles into truth a shrewd insight concerning human nature; *avunculus meus*, my uncle, *et suis libris*, both in his books, *et tuis*, and in yours (vi. 16. 3)—the two Plinys and Tacitus are all in this endeavor together with pride of (last) place going to Tacitus.

Asyndeton, ordering of words, phrases, or clauses without conjunctions or disjunctions: *complectitur consolatur hortatur*, embraces consoles heartens (vi. 16. 12); *orare hortari iubere*, begs cajoles orders (vi. 20. 12)—the piling up of finite verbs in the first example and of infinitives in the second dramatizes the pathos of these human interactions.

Chiasmus, components of a phrase or clause arranged in an A–B–B–A pattern: *candida interdum, interdum sordida,* white sometimes, sometimes dark (vi. 16. 6)—the chiasmus (color adjective–temporal adverb–same temporal adverb–different color adjective) builds suspense: one wonders, though maybe suspects, what will be opposed to "white;" *me cum omnibus, omnia mecum,* me with everything, everything with me (vi. 20. 17)—Pliny and everything are perforce all jumbled up and will perish together.

Polyptoton, repetition of a word's root inside nearby words: *morti eius si celebretur a te immortalem gloriam,* the deathless glory of his death (vi. 16. 1)—the death of Pliny's uncle in and of itself will stay glorious because of Tacitus's writing about it; *tum se quieti dedit, et quievit verissimo quidem somno,* gave himself over to quiet and was quiet indeed in very real sleep (vi. 16. 13)—Pliny's uncle's carelessness during this dire time foreshadows, perhaps, the worry-free quiet of death; *aut facere scribenda aut scribere legenda,* or to do what is worth writing or to write what is worth reading (vi. 16. 3)—the different forms of "write" is an elegant and succinct way, particularly appropriate in an introduction, for Pliny to comment on his purpose; moreover, the mix of chiasmus and synchysis (cf. infra) here, focuses attention on the contrast Pliny wants to set up between "doing" and "reading."

Synchysis, components of a phrase or clause arranged in an A–B–A–B pattern: *nunc huc nunc illuc,* now hither, now thither (vi. 16. 15)—the singsong of the interlock (temporal

adverb–spatial adverb–same temporal adverb–different spatial adverb) makes the buildings' shakes audible; *apud illum
... ratio rationem, apud alios timorem timor vicit*, with him
... reason beats out reason, with the others ... fear beats
out fear (vi. 16. 6)—the two contrasts (Uncle Gaius vs. others,
reason vs. fear) collide in this spectacular double interlock.

Some examples at sentence level

Historic Present tense, forcing of verbs into the present
tense to enliven narrative of events in the past: *regebat ...
mater indicat ... gustaverat ... studebatque, poscit soleas,
ascendit ... conspici poterat*, was in charge ... mother points
out ... had had lunch ... was reading ... puts on sandals,
goes up ... could be viewed (vi. 16. 5); *egrediebatur domo ...
accipit codicullos ... villa subiacebat ... vertit consilium ...
quod incohaverat ... obit ... deducit*, was leaving the house
... receives a note ... house lay under ... changes his plan ...
what had begun ... ends up ... boards (vi. 16. 12); *excedere
visum (est) ... sequitur vulgus ... consistimus ... vehicula
iusseramus ... agebantur ... videbamus*, decided to leave ...
crowd follows ... we make a halt ... vehicles we had ordered
... were going ... we saw (vi. 20. 7-9); *invaluit ... inrumpit
... surgebam ... residimus ... dividebat*, grew strong ...
bursts ... was rising ... we sit down ... separated (vi. 16. 12).
Generally intolerable in good English prose because consid-
ered hard on the mind's perception of meaning, a sudden
switching back and forth between—or a fading in and out
of, or a foray into and a retreat from—different tenses in
the ancient languages was acceptable, common, and effec-
tive. The technique allowed authors subtle fluidity in the

narrative with the action to be spotlit on the stage of their story positioned—popped, it seems sometimes to modern readers—into the present. The effect in English can be felt in oral storytelling when moments of melodrama, though in the past, so easily leap over into the present. With Pliny, this reader has found that record of happenstance, i.e. a mere act or fact, usually, is expressed by one of the past tenses, whereas record of participation, usually, is present, i.e. when Pliny is recording his own or another's involvement in an event or when he is reliving an action himself or vicariously through one of his sources. In the examples above, the excitement such tense change generates is easily imagined.

Isocolon, components of equal or near-equal length in a clause or sentence: *Quamvis enim pulcherrimarum clade terrarum, ut populi ut urbes memorabili casu, quasi semper victurus OCCIDERIT, quamvis ipse plurima opera et mansura condiderit, multum tamen perpetuitati eius scriptorum tuorum aeternitas addet.* Although in the destruction of most beautiful lands ... as it were to live forever PERISHED, although ... (vi. 16. 2). This extraordinary sentence, divided by the anaphora of *quamvis* (although), contains the dreadful word *occiderit* (perished) at its very center, with fourteen words beforehand referring to the perishing of the countryside near Naples and with fifteen words afterward referring to the perishing of Pliny's uncle: both land and man *perished!*

Omission of verb, to hasten or vivify events in narrative: *Iam hora diei prima, et adhuc dubius et quasi languidus dies.* Now the first hour of day, and still a doubtful and sort of slow day. *Iam quassatis circumiacentibus tectis, quamquam in aperto loco, angusto tamen, magnus et certus ruinae metus.*

Now with surrounding buildings shaken, although in open space, nevertheless narrow, great and sure the fear of ruin. (vi. 20. 6). The pithy verblessness of these sentences, bizarre in English, together with the anaphora of "now," renders static or timeless the dawn and the circumstances of the catastrophe's second day, which paradox injects a note of unreality into the narrative, and unreal is surely how Pliny and his mother must have felt at the time.

*   *   *

It is our intention that readers gain as full an appreciation of Pliny's story as possible—hence the illustrations, which reflect what is going on in the text on the page on which it is going on, and hence, too, the translations, which deflect as much as possible those forces of a modern language that might get in the way of savoring Pliny's Latinity, even at the occasional cost of comely English. A translator confronts hopefully the delicacies if not the preciosities of style described above and in the Endnotes; the adapter compromises necessarily and constantly in rendering them. The goal here is to attain the same configuration of words and nicety of diction that Pliny produces with such poise, but the priority has always been at the least to impel and, with some luck, to compel this admirable writer's thought.

THE LETTERS

LIBRI VI EPISTULA 16

C. Plinius Tacito suo s. —

1 Petis ut tibi avunculi mei exitum scribam, quo verius tradere posteris possis. Gratias ago; nam video morti eius si celebretur a te immortalem gloriam esse propositam. 2 Quamvis enim pulcherrimarum clade terrarum, ut populi ut urbes memorabili casu, quasi semper victurus occiderit, quamvis ipse plurima opera et mansura condiderit, multum tamen perpetuitati eius

BOOK VI, LETTER 16

Gaius Pliny greets his friend Tacitus —

1 You ask that I write you about my uncle's fate so that you can transmit to posterity what really happened. Thank you for asking as I envision the deathless glory of his death to be assured if celebrated by you. 2 Although he perished in the ruination of this most beautiful of regions, as whole communities and cities did in the unforgettable calamity, he will as it were live forever.

scriptorum tuorum aeternitas addet. 3 Equidem beatos puto, quibus deorum munere datum est aut facere scribenda aut scribere legenda, beatis﹣ simos vero quibus utrumque. Horum in numero avunculus meus et suis libris et tuis erit. Quo libentius suscipio, deposco etiam quod iniungis.

~~~~~~~~~~~~~~~~~~~~~~~~~~~~~~~~~~

Even though he wrote many works sure to last, nevertheless the immortality of your writings will add greatly to the survival of his. 3 For my part, I consider blessed those who, by a gift of the gods, do what is worth recording or record what is worth reading. Very blessed indeed are those who do both. In this number my uncle, because of his books as well as yours, will be counted. All the more freely, therefore, do I undertake and even demand as my own the task you now impose.

4 Erat Miseni classemque imperio praesens regebat. Nonum kal. Septembres hora fere septima
mater mea indicat ei adparere nubem inusitata
et magnitudine et specie. 5 Usus ille sole, mox
frigida, gustaverat iacens studebatque; poscit
soleas, ascendit locum ex quo maxime miracu-
lum illud conspici poterat. Nubes—incertum
procul intuentibus ex quo monte (Vesuvium
fuisse postea cognitum est)—oriebatur, cuius
similitudinem et formam non alia magis arbor
quam pinus expresserit. 6 Nam longissimo ve-

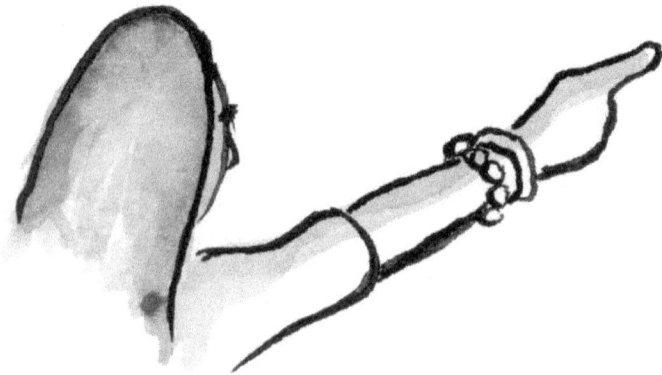

4 He was at Misenum in command of the imperial fleet. About one o'clock on August 24, my mother points out to him a cloud extraordinary in size and shape. 5 He had taken a sunbath, then a cool plunge and light lunch, and was lying down reading. He asks for his sandals and goes up to a spot from which this amazing sight could best be viewed. A cloud—to those watching at a distance it was uncertain from what mountain, but later it was learned to have been Vesuvius—was rising. Its shape resembled a stone-pine more than any other tree. 6 For having risen up in the guise of a very long trunk, it spread out at the top in

lut trunco elata in altum quibusdam ramis diffundebatur, credo quia recenti spiritu evecta, dein senescente eo destituta aut etiam pondere suo victa in latitudinem vanescebat, candida interdum, interdum sordida et maculosa prout terram ciner-emve sustulerat. 7 Magnum propiusque noscendum ut eruditissimo viro visum. Iubet liburnicam aptari; mihi si venire una vellem facit copiam; respondi studere

kinds of branches because, I think, driven out by the crater's recent explosion then left adrift by flagging force or actually overcome by its own weight, the thing began to dissipate sideways, white sometimes, other times dark and blotchy, depending on whether it had picked up earth or ash. 7 This great phenomenon, once glimpsed by such a learned man, begged to be examined more closely. My uncle orders a galley readied. As for me, he makes room in case I should wish to come along. I told him I would rather study and, as it

me malle, et forte ipse quod scriberem dederat.
8 Egrediebatur domo; accipit codicillos Rectinae
Tasci imminenti periculo exterritae (nam villa
eius subiacebat, nec ulla nisi navibus fuga): ut se
tanto discrimini eriperet orabat. 9 Vertit ille consilium et quod studioso animo incohaverat obit
maximo. Deducit quadriremes, ascendit ipse non
Rectinae modo sed multis (erat enim frequens
amoenitas orae) laturus auxilium. 10 Properat illuc unde alii fugiunt, rectumque cursum recta

happened, what I was writing he himself had assigned me. 8 Just as he was leaving the house, he receives a note from Tascus's wife Rectina, terrified by the imminent threat, since her villa lay close to the mountain and there was no escape except by boat: she was begging him to snatch her from such great peril. 9 He changes his plan, and what had started out in scientific spirit ends up heroic. He launches quadriremes and gets on board himself, intending to take aid not only to Rectina but to many who crowded our charming coast. 10 He hastens toward what others are flee-ing, and he keeps the steering oars straight—and

gubernacula in periculum tenet adeo solutus metu ut omnes illius mali motus omnes figuras ut deprenderat oculis dictaret enotaretque. 11 Iam navibus cinis incidebat, quo propius accederent, calidior et densior; iam pumices etiam nigrique et ambusti et fracti igne lapides; iam vadum subitum ruinaque montis litora obstantia. Cunctatus paulum an retro flecteret, mox gubernatori ut ita

straight into danger his course—completely fear-less so as to dictate and record all the activities and all the aspects of this extraordinary evil as he took them in with his own eyes. 11 Now, ash began to fall on the boats, the hotter and heavier the closer they got; now, bits of pumice and even rocks, blackened and broken and scorched by fire; now, a shoal that had arisen and debris from the mountain made the shore unapproachable. After a moment's hesitation as to whether he should turn back, he said to the captain who was

faceret monenti "Fortes" inquit "fortuna iuvat:
Pomponianum pete." 12 Stabiis erat diremptus
sinu medio (nam sensim circumactis curvatisque
litoribus mare infunditur); ibi quamquam non‑
dum periculo adpropinquante, conspicuo tamen
et cum cresceret proximo, sarcinas contulerat in
naves, certus fugae si contrarius ventus resedis‑
set. Quo tunc avunculus meus secundissimo

warning him that he should, "Fortune favors the brave, head for Pomponianus!" [12] This gentleman was at Stabiae, cut off by an intervening cove, for little by little the sea is pouring in on the curved and rounded coastline. There, with the danger not yet close but clearly evident nonetheless, and, should it increase, very close indeed, Pomponianus had put bundles aboard boats, resolved on escape if the onshore wind would only drop. But having sailed in right then on this (for him favorable) breeze, my uncle hugs

invectus, complectitur trepidantem consolatur hortatur, utque timorem eius sua securitate leniret, deferri in balineum iubet; lotus accubat cenat, aut hilaris aut (quod aeque magnum) similis hilari. 13 Interim e Vesuvio monte pluribus in locis latissimae flammae altaque incendia relucebant, quorum fulgor et claritas tenebris

the distraught man, consoles him and heartens him and, in order to put him at ease by his own sense of security, directs that he be taken to the baths. Once bathed, he reclines at table and dines in jolly spirits or—what is equally grand—like one who is so. 13 Meanwhile, in many places very broad banners of flame and high-flying cinders shone from Mount Vesuvius, their gleam and brilliance intensified by the darkness of the

noctis excitabatur. Ille agrestium trepidatione ignes relictos desertasque villas per solitudinem ardere in remedium formidinis dictitabat. Tum se quieti dedit et quievit verissimo quidem somno; nam meatus animae, qui illi propter amplitudinem corporis gravior et sonantior erat, ab eis qui limini obversabantur audiebatur. 14 Sed area ex qua diaeta adibatur ita iam cinere mixtisque pumicibus oppleta surrexerat, ut si longior in

night. To allay fear, Uncle kept saying that it was the abandoned hearths and deserted homesteads of frightened peasants that were burning untended. Then he gave himself over to some rest and must have fallen into a deep sleep, for his respiration, which was deep and loud due to the bulk of his body, was heard by those on watch at the door. 14 But the courtyard from which his suite was entered had filled up already to such an extent with ash and pumice mixed together that, if he lingered in the room, leaving would

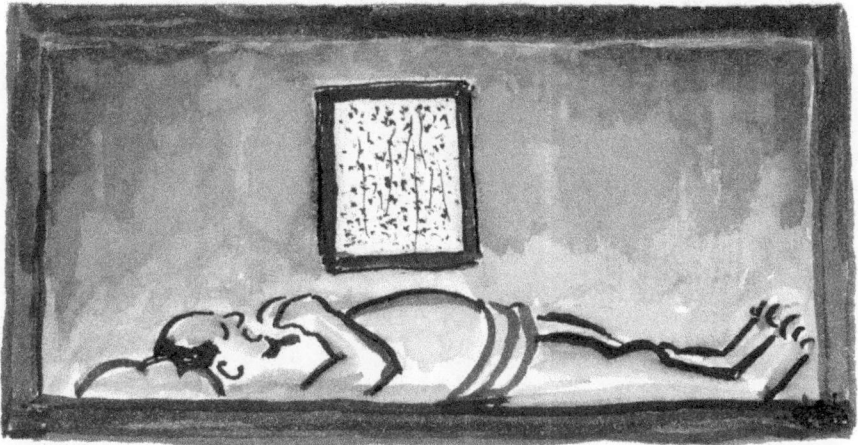

cubiculo mora, exitus negaretur. Excitatus procedit, seque Pomponiano ceterisque qui pervigilaverant reddit. 15 In commune consultant, intra tecta subsistant an in aperto vagentur. Nam crebris vastisque tremoribus tecta nutabant, et quasi emota sedibus suis nunc huc nunc illuc abire aut referri videbantur. 16 Sub dio rursus quamquam levium exesorumque pumicum casus

prove impossible. Roused from his slumbers, my uncle goes out and rejoins Pomponianus and the others who had stayed awake. 15 They discuss whether to stay under cover or venture out into the open. For buildings kept swaying with huge and frequent tremors and seemed to move back and forth, now this way, now that, as if shaken from their foundations. 16 Outside, on the other hand, a rain of pumice, though light and porous, was viewed with alarm; a comparison

metuebatur, quod tamen periculorum collatio elegit; et apud illum quidem ratio rationem, apud alios timorem timor vicit. Cervicalia capitibus imposita linteis constringunt; id munimentum adversus incidentia fuit. [17] Iam dies alibi, illic nox omnibus noctibus nigrior densiorque; quam tamen faces multae variaque lumina solvebant. Placuit egredi in litus, et ex proximo adspicere,

of the dangers, nevertheless, dictated the "stay outside" option. In my uncle's eyes, certainly, one reason prevailed over its alternative; as for the rest of the company, one kind of fear merely annulled another. They place cushions on their heads and tie them up with cloth strips—this was their bulwark against the falling rock. 17 By now, it was daytime elsewhere; there, a night blacker and denser than all nights was diffused

ecquid iam mare admitteret; quod adhuc vastum et adversum permanebat. 18 Ibi super abiectum linteum recubans semel atque iterum frigidam aquam poposcit hausitque. Deinde flammae flammarumque praenuntius odor sulpuris alios in fugam vertunt, excitant illum. 19 Innitens servulis duobus adsurrexit et statim concidit, ut ego colligo, crassiore caligine spiritu obstructo,

only by many torches and various lights. It was
decided to walk out to the shore and ascertain
from close up whether the sea would at last ad-
mit of departure; it remained wild and contrary
still. 18 There my uncle, lying down on a spread
sail, demanded and gulped cold water, once and
then again. At this point, flames and the herald
of flames, an odor of sulphur, put the others to
flight and roused him. 19 He got up by leaning on
two slave boys and immediately fell down again,

clausoque stomacho qui illi natura invalidus et
angustus et frequenter aestuans erat. 20 Ubi
dies redditus (is ab eo quem novissime viderat
tertius), corpus inventum integrum inlaesum
opertumque ut fuerat indutus: habitus corporis
quiescenti quam defuncto similior.

as I suspect, on account of the thick fumes, his stifled breath, and blocked windpipe, which was by nature weak and narrow and regularly inflamed. 20 When day came round again—the third daylight from the last he had seen—my uncle's body was found in one piece, unhurt, and clothed as he had been. He looked more like a man sleeping than like one who was dead.

21 Interim Miseni ego et mater—sed nihil ad historiam, nec tu aliud quam de exitu eius scire voluisti. Finem ergo faciam. 22 Unum adiciam, omnia me quibus interfueram quaeque statim, cum maxime vera memorantur, audieram per-secutum. Tu potissima excerpes; aliud est enim epistulam aliud historiam, aliud amico aliud omnibus scribere. Vale.

21 Meanwhile, at Misenum, Mother and I . . . but this is nothing for history, and you did not wish to know anything except about my uncle's death, so I shall make an end. 22 Let me add that I alone followed up with everything in which I had been involved as well as, immediately, with everything I had heard, when truth is most apt to be related. You will excerpt what is most important. Writing a letter is one thing, history another; the first is for a friend, the other for everybody. Farewell.

LIBRI VI EPISTULA 20

C. Plinius Tacito suo s. —

1 Ais te adductum litteris quas exigenti tibi de morte avunculi mei scripsi, cupere cognoscere, quos ego Miseni relictus (id enim ingressus abruperam) non solum metus verum etiam casus pertulerim. "Quamquam animus meminisse horret, . . . / incipiam." 2 Profecto avunculo ipse reliquum tempus studiis (ideo enim remanseram) impendi; mox balineum cena somnus inquietus et

BOOK VI, LETTER 20

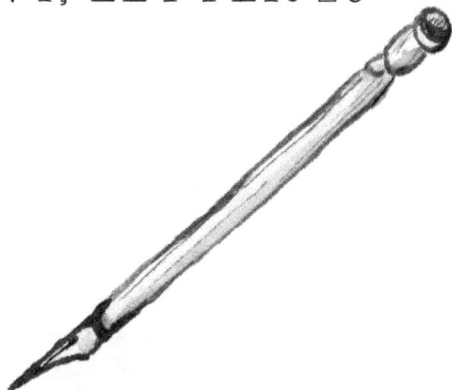

Gaius Pliny greets his friend Tacitus —

1 You say you were moved by the letter I wrote at your request concerning the death of my uncle and now wish to learn about the fears as well as the misfortunes that I experienced left behind at Misenum, for these I had only touched upon before breaking off. "Although the mind recoils from recollection, I will begin." 2 Once Uncle was gone, I studied a while longer; after all, this

brevis. 3 Praecesserat per multos dies tremor terrae, minus formidolosus quia Campaniae solitus;
illa vero nocte ita invaluit, ut non moveri omnia
sed verti crederentur. 4 Inrupit cubiculum meum
mater; surgebam invicem, si quiesceret excitatu-
rus. Resedimus in area domus, quae mare a tectis

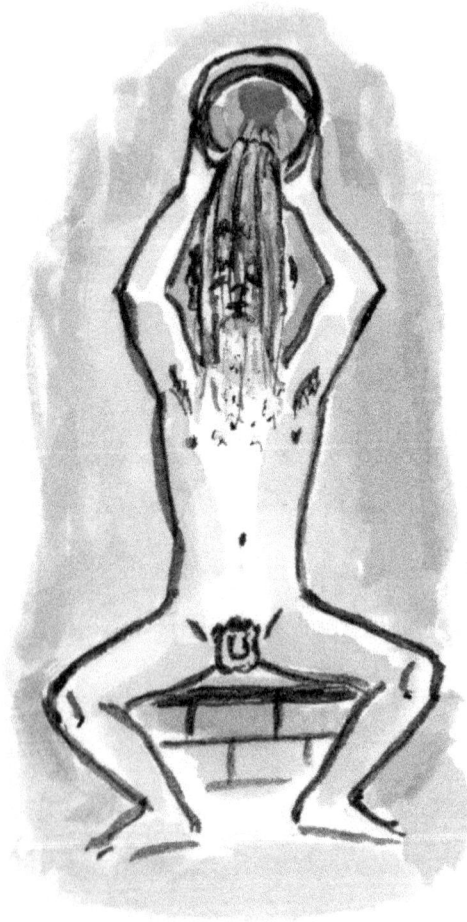

is why I had stayed behind. Later I had a bath, some supper, a brief and restless sleep. 3 For many days there had been a trembling of the earth, not very alarming because common in the Campania. That night, however, it got so strong everything was thought not to be shaking but spinning. 4 Mother bursts into my room; I was getting up myself with the intention of rousing her in case she was still asleep. We install ourselves in the small yard that separated the

modico spatio dividebat. 5 Dubito, constantiam vocare an imprudentiam debeam (agebam enim duodevicesimum annum): posco librum Titi Livi, et quasi per otium lego atque etiam ut coeperam excerpo. Ecce amicus avunculi qui nuper ad eum ex Hispania venerat, ut me et matrem sedentes, me vero etiam legentem videt, illius patientiam securitatem meam corripit. Nihilo segnius ego intentus in librum. 6 Iam hora diei prima, et

sea from our house. 5 I wonder whether I should call this dedication or foolhardiness, since I was seventeen: I ask for my book of Livy and, as if with all the time in the world, read and even take notes, as I had already begun to do. Then, lo and behold, Uncle's friend who had recently come from Spain sees Mother and me in chairs with me actually reading; he rebukes her apathy and my lack of concern, for in no way was I a sluggard when intent on a book. 6 Now it was dawn and daylight itself still in doubt, as if inert.

adhuc dubius et quasi languidus dies. Iam
quassatis circumiacentibus tectis, quamquam in
aperto loco, angusto tamen, magnus et certus
ruinae metus. 7 Tum demum excedere oppido
visum; sequitur vulgus attonitum, quodque in
pavore simile prudentiae, alienum consilium suo
praefert, ingentique agmine abeuntes premit
et impellit. 8 Egressi tecta consistimus. Multa

Now, too, the surrounding buildings had been undermined, the open space we were in was narrow, and general collapse was a great and immediate fear. 7 Only then did we decide to leave. A mob of common folk follows in a daze, preferring another's plan to their own, which mindset in terror passes for prudence; in a large stream they press and push us on. 8 Once beyond the

ibi miranda, multas formidines patimur. Nam vehicula quae produci iusseramus, quamquam in planissimo campo, in contrarias partes agebantur, ac ne lapidibus quidem fulta in eodem vestigio quiescebant. 9 Praeterea mare in se resorberi et tremore terrae quasi repelli videbamus. Certe processerat litus, multaque animalia maris siccis harenis detinebat. Ab altero latere nubes atra

covered areas, we come to a halt: there we take in many things to be marveled at, many fearsome horrors. The carts we had ordered, though on very flat ground, were moving every which way and even when braced with rocks would not stay put. 9 Moreover, we beheld the sea suck back on itself, as if repelled by the earth's trembling. Undoubtedly the shoreline had receded and left behind many sea creatures on dry sand. On the

et horrenda, ignei spiritus tortis vibratisque discursibus rupta, in longas flammarum figuras dehiscebat; fulguribus illae et similes et maiores erant. 10 Tum vero idem ille ex Hispania amicus acrius et instantius "Si frater" inquit "tuus, tuus avunculus vivit, vult esse vos salvos; si periit, superstites voluit. Proinde quid cessatis evadere?" Respondimus non commissuros nos ut de salute illius incerti nostrae consuleremus. 11 Non moratus ultra proripit se effusoque cursu

bay's other side a cloud, black and beetling, rent by shimmering zigzags of fiery breath, would split open onto far reaches of flame, like lightning but larger. 10 At this point, the same friend from Spain spoke sharply and urgently to us. "If your brother," he said, "and your uncle lives, he wishes you safe; if he has perished, he wanted you to survive. Why then do you do nothing to escape?" We reply that we will not make plans for our own safety while uncertain of Uncle's. 11 Delaying no longer, he betakes himself off at full speed and escapes danger. Not much later,

periculo aufertur. Nec multo post illa nubes descendere in terras, operire maria; cinxerat Capreas et absconderat, Miseni quod procurrit abstulerat. 12 Tum mater orare hortari iubere, quoquo modo fugerem; posse enim iuvenem, se et annis et corpore gravem bene morituram, si mihi causa mortis non fuisset. Ego contra salvum me nisi una non futurum; dein manum

the cloud descends to earth and covers the sea: it had encircled and concealed Capri and obscured the headland of Misenum. 12 Then Mother begs, cajoles, orders me to flee by any manner whatsoever, since as a young man, she says, I am able to do so, while she who is heavy in years and body will die well, knowing she has not been the cause of my death. I reply that I shall not be safe unless we are safe together; next, I take her

eius amplexus addere gradum cogo. Paret aegre
incusatque se, quod me moretur. 13 Iam cinis,
adhuc tamen rarus. Respicio: densa caligo ter-
gis imminebat, quae nos torrentis modo infusa
terrae sequebatur. "Deflectamus" inquam "dum
videmus, ne in via strati comitantium turba in
tenebris obteramur." 14 Vix consideramus, et
nox non qualis inlunis aut nubila, sed qualis in
locis clausis lumine exstincto. Audires ululatus

hand and force her to hasten; she complies re-
luctantly and faults herself for holding me back.
13 Presently there is ash, though still sparse. I
look back: a smoky murk loomed behind, and it
kept following us, poured out like flowing earth.
"Let's turn aside," I say, "while we can see lest
we be knocked down on the road by this crowd
and crushed in the darkness." 14 We had hardly
settled ourselves when there arrived a night
not of moonless and cloudy quality but like
that within closed-up places when the lamp has
been extinguished. You could hear the wailing

feminarum, infantum quiritatus, clamores vi-
rorum; alii parentes alii liberos alii coniuges
vocibus requirebant, vocibus noscitabant; hi
suum casum, illi suorum miserabantur; erant
qui metu mortis mortem precarentur; 15 multi
ad deos manus tollere, plures nusquam iam deos
ullos aeternamque illam et novissimam noctem
mundo interpretabantur. Nec defuerunt qui fic-
tis mentitisque terroribus vera pericula augerent.

~~~~~~~~~~~~~~~~~~~~~~~~~~~~~~~~~~~~~~

of women, the bawling of infants, the shouts of
men; some were lifting their voices for parents,
some for children, others for spouses, while try-
ing to make out their relations' voices. One group
bewailed its own misfortune, another that of its
family. There were those who in fear of death
prayed for it; 15 many raised their hands to the
gods, many more professed there were gods no
longer and that this night was the world's last,
and everlasting. Nor was there lacking those
who increased real risk with fictive terror; others declared falsely, but at the expense of the

Aderant qui Miseni illud ruisse illud ardere falso sed credentibus nuntiabant. 16 Paulum reluxit, quod non dies nobis sed adventantis ignis indicium videbatur. Et ignis quidem longius substitit; tenebrae rursus cinis rursus, multus et gravis. Hunc identidem adsurgentes excutiebamus; operti alioqui atque etiam oblisi pondere essemus. 17 Possem gloriari non gemitum mihi, non vocem parum fortem in tantis periculis

credulous, that one section of Misenum had sunk and another was burning. 16 It grew somewhat lighter, yet this seemed to us not daylight but a sign of advancing fire. The fire in fact stayed rather far back; once again darkness descended, again ash, thick and heavy. We got up time after time to shake it off; otherwise, we would have been covered, even smothered, under its weight. 17 I might boast that neither groan nor whine escaped me in such perils except that I had

excidisse, nisi me cum omnibus, omnia mecum perire misero, magno tamen mortalitatis solacio credidissem. 18 Tandem illa caligo tenuata quasi in fumum nebulamve discessit; mox dies verus; sol etiam effulsit, luridus tamen qualis esse cum deficit solet. Occursabant trepidantibus adhuc oculis mutata omnia altoque cinere tamquam nive obducta. 19 Regressi Misenum curatis ut-cumque corporibus suspensam dubiamque noc-tem spe ac metu exegimus. Metus praevalebat; nam et tremor terrae perseverabat, et plerique lymphati terrificis vaticinationibus et sua et

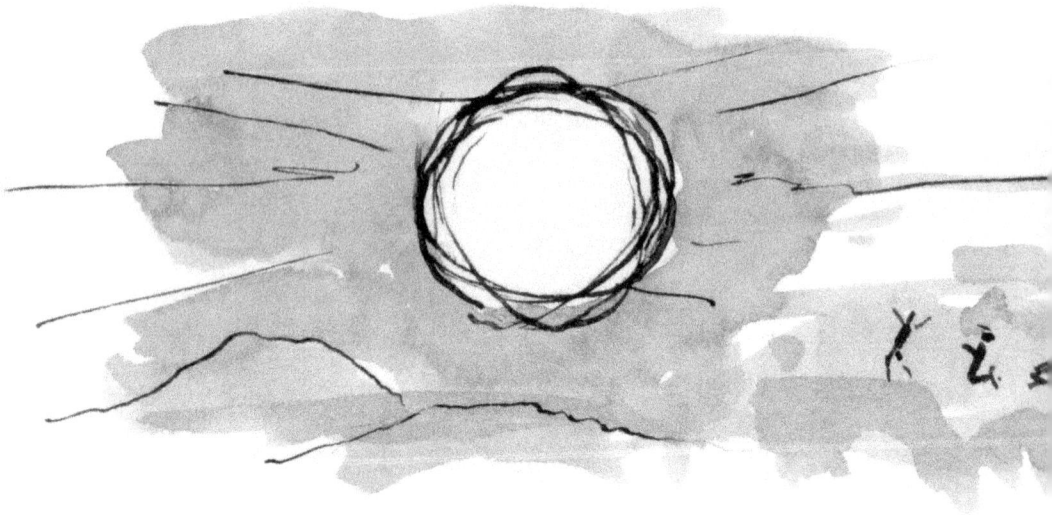

believed I was perishing with everything and everything with me—in the paltry yet powerful consolation of mortality. 18 Finally, the gloom thinned and trailed off, as it were, into smoke or cloud: next there was genuine daylight; the sun even shone forth, though eerily, as during an eclipse. What met our still quavering eyes was this—everything changed, covered in deep ash like snow. 19 We returned to Misenum and, with our bodies cared for however they might, spent in hope and fear a suspenseful and uncertain night. Fear prevailed, for the trembling of

aliena mala ludificabantur. 20 Nobis tamen ne tunc quidem, quamquam et expertis periculum et exspectantibus, abeundi consilium, donec de avunculo nuntius. Haec nequaquam historia digna non scripturus leges et tibi scilicet qui requisisti imputabis, si digna ne epistula quidem videbuntur. Vale.

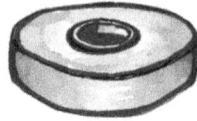

the earth continued, and many frantic people were making a mockery of their own and others' woes with frightful prophecies. 20 Mother and I, however, even then had no thought of leaving in spite of the peril we had been through, and the danger we still faced, until word should arrive from Uncle. These things, by no means worthy of history, you will read but not recount, and you, who after all did demand them, will blame yourself if they appear worthy not even of a letter. Farewell.

ENDNOTES

Pliny the Younger's personal letters, after some sprucing up, were arranged by the author himself and published in nine books between the years 100 and 109; a tenth book contains his official correspondence with the emperor Trajan and is written in a less polished style. The only other work of this Pliny that survives is the so-called *Panegyricus Traiani*, a more-or-less obligatory paean to the emperor, highly stylized and fulsome in modern ears, for appointing him *legatus* in Bithynia-Pontus.

The production of books was beginning to change during the first century with various circumstances promoting the manufacture of the *codex* or assemblage of cut papyrus sheets sewn between wooden covers; this *codex*, improved upon insofar only as the manipulation of natural resources and human ingenuity progressed, has been the norm since. Nevertheless, it is most likely that Pliny the Younger's letters were sent to their recipients and subsequently copied for the market in the centuries-old fashion of a *volumen* or roll of papyrus wound round a stick, which method of publication was still the more usual during his lifetime. The text would have been written with pen and ink in three-inch columns and read by unwinding the scroll counterclockwise, the *recto* or written-on side facing in. Incredible to modern readers is the fact that there was no word separation nor capitalization nor paragraphing and only the scantiest of punctuation. The books of Pliny the Younger and those of his uncle Pliny the Elder would ordinarily have been read aloud by a slave to his master, perhaps at dinner in company with wife and friends, as the nephew records in one of his letters (ix. 99. 4).

The earliest surviving copies in manuscript of the younger Pliny's work date from the ninth century, and a collation of mss. formed the *editio princeps*, which was printed at Venice in 1471; the version used here is based on a new recension, the text of which forms part of the Oxford Classical Texts (OCT) series: C. Plini Caecili Secundi *Epistularum libri decem*, ed. R. A. B. Mynors, Oxford 1963. Lexical authority throughout is that of the *Oxford Latin Dictionary*, ed. P. G. W. Glare, Oxford 1982.

The Roman numeral on the left of the line above each note (vi) refers to the sixth book of Pliny's collected work, whence both these letters come; the Arabic numbers attached to this refer to the individual letter and to the "chapter" or small section, often only a sentence or two long, wherein the glossed word or passage appears. The number to the far right identifies the page on which the word or passage occurs in the present volume.

vi. 16. salutation   21

greets   The *s.* in the Latin stands for *salutem*, the accusative case of *salus* (greetings) with an understood "d." for *dicit* (speaks), a third-person verb whose subject is *C. Plinius* (a "C" not a "G," though the name was pronounced GUY-oos and when spelled out in full also began with a "G"). The formula includes the word *suo* (his), which corresponds to our "dear." Thus the Latin means something like "Pliny sends greetings to his good friend Tacitus." The sixteenth and twentieth letters of Book VI were composed, it is worth repeating, twenty-five years after the events they recount.

vi. 16. 1   21

if celebrated by you   in Tacitus's great *Historiae*, then a work in progress, concerning life and politics in the Rome of the first century CE; less than half this magnum opus survives, and if Tacitus made use of Pliny the Younger's reportage, he would have done so in those portions that dealt with events after 70, which portions are now entirely lost.

deathless glory of his death   an example of the dramatizing word play, odd or annoying to modern taste as it is, which Pliny the Younger could produce.

vi. 16. 2   21

whole communities   which rendering may not be quite right for *populi*, a word used for "peoples" or "races" or, simply, "nations;" possibly Pliny the Younger hyperbolizes mock-grandly.

and cities   viz. Pompeii, Herculaneum, Stabiae.

the immortality of your writings   because Tacitus was recognized even in his own day as the master of Roman history.

vi. 16. 4   25

Misenum   a navy town and the cape on which it was founded, known in Italian as *Miseno*, memorializes the legendary trumpeter Misenus who accompanied Aeneas and drowned off the coast of the Campania (Italian *Campagna*) at the northwestern tip of the curve that forms the Bay of Naples, a place of great beauty still and dotted with villas.

in command of the imperial fleet   a purely administrative command granted to Pliny the Elder shortly before his death as an honorarium by the emperor Vespasian, whose son, the future emperor Titus, this Pliny had accompanied on a visit to Germany in 57. Naples was the headquarters of the Roman fleet for the western coast of Italy, Ravenna that for the eastern.

About one o'clock on August 24   rendered in Latin according to Roman custom as "on the ninth day (counting inclusively) before the Kalends (i.e. the first day) of September about the seventh hour (from sunrise)."

mother points out   the first instance in these two letters of the Historic Present.

taken a sunbath   which activity was unusual for a Roman aristocrat, as only farmers or slaves in ancient Italy were adepts of sunshine. Pliny the Elder must have lain out in the sun for medicinal purposes, probably to alleviate arthritis or some like ailment.

stone pine   a pine *(Pinus pinea)* of southern Europe, with a wide-spreading, flat-topped head.

vi. 16. 7   27

a galley   the *liburnica*, a light swift vessel, named after the Liburnian pirates of Dalmatia.

orders ... should wish ... makes ... told   a characteristic mishmash of tenses which has the effect of rousing a reader's sense of event; what is in the present *(facit, makes)* enlivens the uncle's gesture; what is in the past *(respondi, told)* makes definite and, in the event, portentous the nephew's reply.

vi. 16. 8   29

exercise he himself had assigned me   which task for a young student then would involve writing out a summary of a notable selection from an esteemed author, in this case, as is specified at vi. 20. 5, a passage from Livy, the most respected historian of early Rome.

76

receives a note   most likely on a *codicillus* (little codex), a small, hinged tablet inlaid with dark wax, into which memos, notes, lists, *aide-mémoire*, etc. were incised with a stylus.

Tascus's wife Rectina   neither husband nor wife is otherwise known; no further reference is made by Pliny the Younger to this poor lady, so it is impossible to tell whether she was saved or not.

vi. 16. 9   29

quadriremes   vessels considerably larger than *liburnicae* with four rowers per compartment on a single deck or, depending on one's interpretation (or imagination), four decks and an undetermined number of rowers.

who crowded   the sudden insertion of this imperfect tense (*erat*), combined with its prime position in the parenthetical clause, renders poignant the volcanic catastrophe inflicted on the coastline's charm—the coast would *no longer* be popular.

vi. 16. 10   31

dictate   to a literate slave, taken along for the purpose.

vi. 16. 11   33

Fortune favors the brave   a favorite proverb of the Romans, worded variously in Latin and found, among other places, in the playwright Terence (*Phormio*, line 203) and in the poet Vergil (*Aeneid*, Book X, line 284).

Pomponianus   presumably another acquaintance of Pliny the Elder's.

vi. 16. 12   33

Stabiae   the present-day Castellamare di Stabia, a town facing Misenum across the entirety of the Bay of Naples and, in both Plinys' day, a resort of the very rich.

vi. 16. 19   45

stifled breath   very likely Pliny the Elder was suffering what today would be diagnosed as a severe asthma attack.

daylight   the word *dies* means a host of things, as does "day" in English, but a quite common use of the word in Latin does not share such ubiquity in English—"daylight." Unless this is understood here, along with inclusive counting, the sentence makes no sense.

Farewell   the usual way of ending a letter; the Romans closed their correspondence as simply as they began it.

I will begin   an elegant quotation from Vergil's *Aeneid* (Book II, line 11), whereby Aeneas braces himself for the sorrowful story he is about to tell Dido concerning the fall of Troy and his own wanderings as a refugee.

studied a while longer   on the task his uncle had given him.

because common in the Campania   earth tremors, yes, were common in the area around Vesuvius, especially after a memorable earthquake in 63; as is now known, however, the volcano had last exploded around 800 BCE, and the ancient Romans would not have suspected that it was still active.

bursts into my room   the first reversion in this letter to the Historic Present and (purely?) coincidental that the same initial use of this verb tense in the sixteenth letter has also for its subject Pliny's mother.

I was seventeen   or as Latin idiom puts it, "I was doing (my) eighteenth year."

Uncle's friend   met, perhaps, when Pliny the Elder was *procurator* or financial administrator of Hispania Tarraconensis, i.e. all but the south and southwest of the Iberian Peninsula, in the early part of the emperor Vespasian's reign, c. 73.

intent on a book though others, arguably more correctly, take *in librum* to mean "on *the* book" (viz. the Livy mentioned below and at vi. 16. 7); lack of definite and indefinite articles in Latin presents English translators with one of their greatest challenges in rendering this ancient language.

vi. 20. 11   61

Capreae known today by its Italian name *Capri*; a picturesque mountain-island in the Tyrrhenian Sea southwest of Naples, famous already in the first century as a locale of luxury, where the emperor Tiberius built a number of large and probably beautiful palaces, all now in ruins.

vi. 20. 15   64

professed … the world's last for there was abroad then a doomsday spirit abetted both by Stoic philosophy, in which eschatology was a common theme and which cast a spell on the educated of the early Empire, and by a popular imagination distressed with the mishaps and misrule of Roman government after Augustus; these "professors" were prophetic, at least, of the sea change that would come to Western culture as the Olympian gods and Greek-based philosophy of various schools succeeded to a Christianity with neo-Platonic ideas predominant and, more or less concurrently, as Rome's frontier enemies grew more menacing.

vi. 20. 20   71

no means worthy of history a strange way, to modern sensibility, to acknowledge fulfilling so faithfully the request of another; this false modesty, offensive though it is to a reader today, is a Roman convention and, perhaps, reflects also genuine shyness on Pliny the Younger's part before the august reputation of Tacitus.

The typefaces used to compose this trade edition of
Vesuvius are Kennerly, Kennerly Italic, and Kennerly
Open Caps. This project would not have been possible
without the generous support of the International
Printing Museum in Carson, California, where museum
docent Luis Garcia devoted many hours on the Linotype
for the deluxe limited edition of the book. Additional
thanks are due to the following persons for help in
elucidating Pliny's text, editing the translator's version,
and encouraging generally the publication of this book:
Max Bates, Gerry McAllister, Kathy Miller, and
Shirley H. Steegmuller.

www.ingramcontent.com/pod-product-compliance
Ingram Content Group UK Ltd.
Pitfield, Milton Keynes, MK11 3LW, UK
UKHW011418281025
8645UKWH00001B/97

9 780615 191317